Empowering
Moments

Shavon Sellers

Unless otherwise indicated, all scripture quotations are taken from the *King James Version* of the Bible.

Empowering Moments!
ISBN 978-1500264543
Copyright © 2014 by Shavon Sellers Ministries

Cover Design by: Danielle Ludy Designs (DanielleLudy.com)

Dedication

This book is dedicated to my biggest supporter, my husband Pastor Clarence L. Seller, Jr. and to my three wonderful children Clarence III, Marlon and Kalyn.

I also dedicate this book to my departed father James Sumler, mother Yvonne Sumler, my sister Mona Lisa Avents, my brother Craig Avents, II., and all of my extended family and friends.

To my other parents, Chief Apostle and Apostle, Clarence L. Sellers, Sr. To my other brother and sister, Calvin and Benita Austin.

Lastly, it's dedicated to each member of Dominion and Mt. Tabor COGIC and to those in the body of Christ that have prayed, supported and assisted me in this journey. I love you all.

Table of Contents

Introduction

$\mathcal{N}$o worries, God's got you! How do I know which way to go? Jesus said – I Am the Way for you to take. How do I know if I can be sure and secure? Jesus said because I Am the Truth. How do I know that I will ever be fulfilled, or ever be satisfied? Jesus said because I Am the Life! Jesus says to you today, I got you, I made you, I know that I Am God. No Worries, I Got You through everything that you experience in your life.

It's Time to Wake Up

Day 1

*Romans 13:11-12 (KJV) **11** And that, knowing the time that now it is high time to awake out of sleep: for now is our salvation nearer than when we believed. **12** The night is far spent, the day is at hand: let us therefore cast off the works of darkness, and let us put on the armour of light.*

*W*hen we are asleep that means we are inactive. That's the job of the enemy to render us asleep, ineffective, having us non- productive, to keep us waddling in our pity parties and stuck in our present circumstances. The enemy wants us to give attention to our problems and struggles and take our focus off of God. But the devil is a liar and a deceiver. We won't allow him to dictate to us how we are going to respond. We must respond to trouble with praise, prayer, and faith in knowing that we have the Victory. So while many of us are waiting for the manifestation, we need to WAKE UP.

I Corinthians 15:34 says *"Awake to Righteousness and sin not: for some have not the knowledge of God: I speak this to your shame."* We must allow the Righteousness of God to dictate our lives daily. From the time you wake in the morning until the time you lay down to rest for the evening.

Awake to Holiness, - we have to fulfill our Kingdom mandates and do that which brings God glory! Proverbs 10:15 says, *"He that gathereth in summer is a wise son, but he that sleepeth in harvest is a son that causeth shame.* We don't want to bring shame to our Father because we are sleeping during Harvest time. Let's get up and go to work!

The Bible says, *"Death and life are in the power of the tongue: and they that love it shall eat the fruit thereof"* (Proverbs 18:21). So every morning, when you wake up, you need to confess that you are free to prosper in every aspect of your life and you will not dwell in bondage.

My Prayer: In the name of Jesus, I declare that no longer will I slumber. But I will wake with praise and faith knowing that I have the victory over all adversaries. I will live a life that is pleasing to God and walk in the authority He has given me to speak as He speaks. I will call everything into existence that God has for me and bind anything that is not for me.

*It's Harvest Time People of God. **AWAKE**. We Have Work To Do*

Life's A Relay Race

Day 2

*Phillippians 3:13-14 (ESV) Brothers, I do not consider that I have made it my own. But one thing I do: forgetting what lies behind and straining forward to what lies ahead, **14** I press on toward the goal for the prize of the upward call of God in Christ Jesus.*

Life is like a relay race. You have to wait with anticipation for a teammate to hand off the baton to you. You can hear your teammates rooting for you to endure the process (the race), and not drop the baton. For if you drop the baton the entire team will lose. So, while waiting you must remain focused on the vision of the team, which is winning. Life is the same way. The relay race is your life. Your teammates are the people that God has divinely connected you with, the ones that are carrying your blessing. But, while waiting, you must remain focused on God and the vision he has given you.

As your teammate is approaching towards you with the baton (your blessings), you have to be properly positioned to receive it. You have to remain in the will of

God, completely focused on him, so that you can receive your blessings (the baton), to complete the race.

Once you receive the baton (your blessings), you can't decide to run off course (the track). You must stay in your lane or you will be disqualified (DQ'd). Life is the same way. You can't receive your blessings and decide you now are going to run off course. You stop going to church, stop praying, and stop reading the Word of God (the Bible). This will result in a DQ from reaching the ultimate goal of Victory. You want God to be able to say, *"Well done, my good and faithful servant. You have been faithful in handling this small amount, so now I will give you many more responsibilities. Let's celebrate together!"(Matthew 25:23 NLT)*

*Everyone is depending on you, YOU CAN DO IT! *

My Prayer: *In the name of Jesus, I thank God for those that He has assigned to my team and for the vision that He has given me. I declare that I will remain focused and stay steadfast as I endure the race.*

Pressure Will Not Defeat Me

Day 3

II Corinthians 4:8-9 (NIV)

8 We are hard pressed on every side, but not crushed; perplexed, but not in despair; 9 persecuted, but not abandoned; struck down, but not destroyed.

The word pressed means to act upon with steadily applied weight or force. For example, grapes in winepress, there is constant weight being applied to the grapes to make the wine. Life can sometimes be the same way. The pressures of life may squeeze us and weigh on us steadily, but with God's grace, we are not utterly crushed.

Pressed can be also defined as moving weight or force in a certain direction or into a certain position. For example, you can be walking through a crowd where people will surround you and literally press against you. In life, the pressures are troubles that will press on every side as if you are in a vice, but you are not crushed. Our situations may look bad, but it's not as bad as it looks. The crushing that we are experiencing is for our good. The pressure is God's way of pulling the oil, or anointing, out of us. In the midst of our crushing situations, we take comfort in knowing that His grace is sufficient for us.

Even one of the most valuable, precious stones, the diamond is created by immense pressure and heat deep underground, which turns Carbon into diamonds. Then they make their way to surface via volcanic magma flows and erosion. So, you are a diamond in the rough!

There is Victory in the crushing (troubles), therefore I will glorify Him in my tribulations

My Prayer: *In the name of Jesus, I thank God for the necessary pressures of life that I must endure to experience the anointing He has bestowed upon me. I pray that He continues to grant me the grace to sustain as I continue to glorify Him in the midst.*

The Devil is After Your Faith

Day 4

Luke 22:32 But I have prayed for thee that thy faith fail not: and when thou art converted strengthen thy brethren.

*J*esus is talking to Peter and letting him know that the enemy wanted to have him and sift him. Jesus did not pray to paralyze the devil. He simply prayed that Peter's faith would not fail.

> **The devil cannot prevail if your faith does not fail.**

Satan is determined to shipwreck and destroy the faith of God's people. The stronger our faith, the greater will be his attack against us.

1). **We walk by Faith** – walking by faith is to walk according to the Word of God. When God asked Abraham to sacrifice his only son, Abraham walked by faith knowing that God didn't bless him to turn around and take it away. It was because of his faith in God, that when he had the knife in his hand, prepared to sacrifice his son that he heard the voice of God saying. "Abraham Stop! Do not hurt your son. You have proven to me your faith and shown how you love me by being willing to sacrifice your son for me. Therefore, I shall bless you and your family, and through you, I shall bless all the nations on the earth". God then provided a lamb for the sacrifice. (*Genesis 22:1-19*)

2). **We live by Faith** – Galatians 3:11 (KJV), But that no man is justified by the law in the sight of God, it is evident; for, The just shall live by faith. What is the meaning of "the just shall live by faith"? The term *just* means "righteous"—an individual whose personality and behavior are acceptable to God. The word *live* means "to be, think, speak, and act." The term *faith* means "love for, always seeking, reliance on, hope in, obedience to, and trust in God."

"The just shall live by faith" is defined as follows: the individual whose personality and behavior are acceptable to what God thinks, speaks, and acts as one who loves, seeks, relies on, hopes in, obeys, and trusts God.

The opposite of the just person is the unrighteous person—the individual whose personality and behavior are not acceptable to God. The opposite of to *live by faith* is to think, speak, and act as one who does not love, seek, rely on, hope in, obey, or trust God. It's pertinent that you rely on and trust in God by living by faith.

3). **We overcome by Faith** – I John 5:4 (ESV), says: "For everyone who has been born of God overcomes the world. And this is the victory that has overcome the world – our faith.

4). **We win by Faith** – Hebrews 6:12 (NLT) says, "Then you will not become spiritually dull and indifferent. Instead, you will follow the example of those who are going to inherit God's promises because of their faith and endurance.

Don't allow your Faith to Fail. We accomplish great things by faith. We enjoy victory over the devil by faith and that is why Satan attacks our Faith! Our faith is a threat to the devil because this is what we use against him and his kingdom. Ephesians 6:16 says that we can quench all the fiery darts of the wicked by faith.

DON'T allow your Faith to Fail

*My **Prayer:** In the name of Jesus, I pray that my faith will not fail and the enemy will not prevail.*

You Have Been Authorized

Day 5

Luke 10:19 (NKJV) Behold, I give you the authority to trample on serpents and scorpions, and over all the power of the enemy, and nothing shall by any means hurt you.

God through his son Jesus Christ has given us authority. He has given us the power to command and to act, and He did this by defeating Satan on the Cross of Calvary as Jesus Christ bore our sins on that cross.

Authority is a right to command. Authority doesn't beg, Authority doesn't ask, but Authority simply commands. We are not told in the word of God to ask God to cast out demons. We are not told to beg demons to come out. But rather, we are told we have the Authority to cast them out. Authority is exercised through our spoken word. The power of life and death are in the spoken word. Proverbs 18:21 *Death and life are in the power of the tongue.*

You have been Authorized...take Authority!

My Prayer: In the name of Jesus, I declare that I will stand and speak boldly against all evil and anything that is not of God, I bind it in the Holy and Magnificent name of Jesus!

Get Up, Dust Yourself Off and Try Again

Day 6

I John 2:1-2 (NKJV) My little children, these things I write to you, so that you may not sin. And if anyone sins, we have an Advocate with the Father, Jesus Christ the righteous. 2 And He Himself is the propitiation for our sins, and not for ours only but also for the whole world.

Lamentations 3:22 Through the Lord's mercies we are not consumed. Because His compassions fail not. 23 They are new every morning; great is Your faithfulness. (NKJV)

𝒯he only thing that keeps us from the steadfast love of the Lord and his mercy is, us. Sometimes, we are unwilling to let go of our sins, or our guilt.

Maybe you feel like…

- ❖ You were not the best parent
- ❖ Came to Christ too late
- ❖ Married the wrong person
- ❖ Lived a life that was unpleasing to God for years

Maybe you deal with guilt because…

- ❖ You abused someone
- ❖ You cheated on your spouse
- ❖ You robbed a bank…. or any such thing…

If you confess your sins, He is faithful to forgive you. Once you confess, God will do the rest.

*Be not afraid to Get Up! Dust
Yourself Off and Try Again.*

My Prayer: In the name of Jesus, I am ask God for forgiveness and I declare that through His forgiveness, I will forgive myself and allow God to do good works within me.

Go Back Again

Day 7

I Kings 18:41 gives an account of the Prophet Elijah declaring that there is a sound of the abundance of rain.

$\mathcal{R}$ain represents refreshing, hydration transmission of knowledge from a higher to a lower. Rain represents God's blessings to us.

Faith enables us to hear the sound of heavy rain in our spirit and enables us to see a cloud the size of a man's hand. Faith does not declare there is nothing, but instead demands of us to "Go Back Again!" Believe God and persevere in prayer, faith and expectancy.

Faith comes by hearing. It is when the Spirit speaks the Word of God in our souls and speaks it with the Spirit of Christ that faith becomes ours. According to Hebrews 11:6... For without Faith it is impossible to please God.

Elijah sent his servant seven times to look toward the sea,

in anticipation of seeing the "promised" rain. Six times he returned with a "nothing" report. Had he not continued to believe and had given up; there would have been no end to the drought and no end to leprosy. But, because Elijah sent his servant that seventh time—the promised abundance of rain began to fall.

The point is: the facts are there, yes, but he kept sending the servant back until what he **saw lined** up with what **he heard!**

Go Back Again!

My Prayer: In the name of Jesus, I declare that I will continue to go back until what I began to see is in direct alignment with what you promised!

Shake Off Discouragement

Day 8

Zechariah 4:6

Then he answered and spake unto me, saying, this is the word of the Lord unto Zerrubbabel, saying not by might, nor by power, but by my spirit, saith the Lord of hosts.

Zerrubbabel was discouraged when things were not going as he had expected, things were not moving as fast as he wanted. As a matter of fact, the project came to a complete stand still. People had left the work of the temple and began to work on their own houses. So God, speaks to Zerubbabel through the prophet Zechariah and he tells him, "look this temple <u>will be built</u> but it will not be by any man's might, nor by his power, but by My Spirit!

God says to you today <u>let me do it!</u> Remove your hand and any resemblance of work you did and let me be God. Shake off discouragement and praise Me in the midst of Rebuilding. Allow me to lead you and guide you. Your weakness is <u>no</u> obstacle for Me. For God says when you're weak that's when I am made strong in your life.

Walk in Joy today, for God is doing it again in you and don't allow discouragement to hinder the process, to hinder the work from being completed.

Philippians 1:6 Being confident of this very thing, that he which hath begun a good work in you will perform it until the day of Jesus Christ. He will perfect it He will carry it on to completion.

> *My Prayer: In the name of Jesus, I declare that I will remove my hand and allow God to move on my behalf in all sectors of my life so that He gets all of the glory for the many blessings that will be bestowed upon me.*

The Blessings of Being Uncomfortable
Called But Uncomfortable

Day 9

*P*eople avoid discomfort. At the first sign of discomfort we run totally in the opposite direction and this factor limits us the most.

Our nature is geared toward comfort and the pursuit of comfort. But the place where God wants us to be is in a place called "uncomfortable". Being comfortable with what's happening in the world our children, our spouses, our friends, in our churches makes us lazy, it removes our stimulation of our influence!

When we are uncomfortable it forces us to totally trust and rely on God! We begin to realize that we can't do it on our own. That's when we come to the realization that it is not about us it has never been about us. It's all about HIM!

Master your Fear of Discomfort and you can take the world for Christ.

My Prayer: In the name of Jesus, I declare that I will transition out of my comfort zone, and enter a place of discomfort, so that I can solely depend upon the mercies of God.

Waiting on the Lord

Day 10

*W*aiting on The Lord is one of the hardest things to do. The world we live in, and our society does not help it because it presents the direct opposite. We live in a day and time of ever increasing impatience and we've grown accustomed to immediate gratification, so everything we do is done fast.

Our prayers are fast, our devotion time is fast, and our church services are fast; so when God doesn't move in our timing or when we feel he should move we get frustrated, we get antsy, our spirits become unsettled. To "wait" means to remain, to trust, to stay, and to put hope or confidence in God, to be in expectation.

> There is a saying that anything that is of Value is worth waiting for. And this is true of the promises of God.

In Acts1: 4 – Before Jesus Christ ascended to heaven, he commanded – he ordered them that they should not leave Jerusalem 'but wait for the promise of the Father." Jesus gave this command to about five hundred bretheren (I

Corinthians 15:6) yet we read that only about 120 continued with prayer & supplication. So, what happened to the other 380 men? Perhaps they got weary and <u>couldn't</u> <u>wait!</u>

- ❖ It's in the **wait** that your strength is renewed.
- ❖ It's in the **wait** that your faith is increased.
- ❖ It's in the **wait** that your character is being strengthened.
- ❖ It's in the **wait** that you build and strengthen your relationship with God.

Isaiah 40:31 - Wait upon The Lord and he shall renew your strength. So stand still and wait and He will do what he needs to do in you and through you!

<u>Waiting is not easy, but it's necessary!</u>

My Prayer: *In the name of Jesus, I declare that I will wait and allow God to manifest in his timing while I gain more strength, faith and character along the way.*

Take Your Thoughts Captive

Day 11

Casting down imaginations (reasoning.) The Word of God must renew our minds. Many of us are in a battle between our head and our hearts and it's called spiritual warfare.

The Bible tells us that our weapons are not carnal or natural. When Paul says, "casting down imaginations..." imaginations are reasoning's which involves our minds. As long as Satan can hold us in the arena of reason he will defeat us in every battle.

So how do we defeat him in every battle? We defeat him by casting down imaginations and reasoning's and bringing every thought captive to the obedience of Jesus.

If the thought does not line up with the Word of God then reject it. We have to believe and think only on what God's Word says!

Our human knowledge is in opposition to what God's word says cast it down and get rid of it. When negative thoughts come, you must bring every thought into captivity to the obedience of the Word of God. We are Believers not Doubters. We have Faith and our faith is in God the Father and our Lord Jesus Christ.

When you are believing God for your healing, reason will tell you that it can't happen. You must believe for Salvation, believing for Restoration, and Believing for Deliverance. Reason will have you thinking, it won't happen, you will not be saved, the situation will never change, and my body will never be healed. So we have to cast down reasoning and any kind of knowledge that exalts itself against the knowledge of God and His word.

> *My Prayer: In the name of Jesus, I bind every thought provoked by the enemy and I decree that every thought and idea will fall into obedience with God.*

What Do You Do When You've Been Blindsided?

Day 12

Job 1:8 (KJV) And the LORD said unto Satan, Hast thou considered my servant Job, that there is none like him in the earth, a perfect and an upright man, one that feareth God, and escheweth evil?

Sometimes you feel like you've been blind-sided by the enemy. Things happen in our life unexpectedly and you begin to question the rules of life like Job did.

Job is blindsided by the enemy, and he did nothing to deserve what he received. His wealth was taken, his family was killed and the Bible says in the 9th chapter that Job says "there is no arbiter between us." Which means there was no official rule on the hit that took place in his life. There was no voice at the moment to answer why? How long? There may be someone now that's asking the same questions, Lord Why? How long? I want to encourage you to take solace, take refuge, and receive strength in the word of God. With Him, you can overcome any and every situation.

Oftentimes you won't have the answers as to why but we stand on the word of God that says "The suffering of this present time is not worthy to be compared to the glory which shall be revealed.

What you are dealing with right now, your natural mind cannot fathom how you're going to make it or endure. But with God we can stand, with God we won't break, and with God we have power over every situation and circumstance. It may not look like or even feel like it, but God is with us and the more the enemy attacks, it will draw us closer to our Father which is in heaven.

My Prayer: In the name of Jesus, I declare that no matter what comes my way and I am blind-sided that I will keep my face towards God and will not waver.

God Needs Us to Fulfill His Plan

Day 13

I Corinthians 1:27 But God hath chosen the foolish things of the world to confound the wise;

Have you ever bought into the lies of the enemy? The lies- you are not good enough, not anointed enough, not smart enough, and not qualified enough… When God calls you for a particular assignment, know that everything you need is available to you. As a matter of fact, He takes these aforementioned things that seem strange about us and uses it. He takes the foolish things to confound the wise. So, having inadequate feelings are normal.

According to Exodus 3:11, Moses is commissioned by God for service which was a major turning point in his life. The commission was to bring the Children of Israel out of Egypt, out of bondage, and out of captivity. And Moses didn't see himself in that light. Just as you, while reading this book are looking at your own inadequacies and feeling insecure about fulfilling the commission that God has placed over your life. Yes, I know the feelings of not feeling important enough or lacking necessary qualities are real.

No More Excuses!

Rehearse what God says about you in his Word. He says he has a plan for you, that you are fearfully and wonderfully made, that you are chosen, and that you are a new creation. **HE LOVES YOU!**

Jeremiah 29:11 For I know the thoughts that I think toward you, saith the LORD, thoughts of peace, and not of evil, to give you an expected end.

> ***My Prayer:*** *In the name of Jesus, I declare that I am fearfully and wonderfully made and I am who God says I am. I am not inadequate nor am I unimportant, but I am a Child of the Most High God and created for a great purpose!*

Dealing with Warfare

Day 14

𝒯he people of God everywhere are under attack. They are experiencing great warfare because it is the enemy's job to take our focus off of our God and look at our problems. He wants us to stop serving, stop believing, stop fasting, stop reading, and start complaining. Proverbs 24:10 says "If thou faint in the day of adversity, your strength is small." Which means if you are slack or lose hope, are weary in the day of distress or trouble, then what you are saying is "I don't believe God."

Two of the most powerful weapons against Satan's attacks are The Bible, the word of God (the Truth) and Prayer. We have to use them both regularly. Yes Satan has been defeated but he and his imps, those demons that work with him are not yet inactive. They are out to destroy us so we need to constantly fight against his attacks by prayer and the Word.

When Jesus was being attacked and being tempted by the enemy he gave him the word and prayed. Jesus told the disciples in Mark 9:29 that some spirits cannot just be cast out but, prayer and fasting are required.

Effective Prayer for Spiritual Warfare starts with Prayer in general. We should begin from a baseline of an active prayer life and not praying from a position of fear but in confidence knowing that we are praying the will of God. The Bible says in I John 5:15 – And we know that he hears us, whatsoever we ask we know that we have the petitions that we desired of Him. Why? Because in verse 14 it says, And this is the confidence that we have in him, that, if we ask anything according to his will he hears us.

We've got to remain persistent & PRAY our way through it!

My Prayers: In the name of the Jesus, I declare that I will pray my way through every storm and test and stand firm in the Word of God.

Lord, I Need Your Help!

Day 15

*W*e have all heard the statement "life happens." I began thinking about this statement. The question I asked myself was, "What do you do when life happens in ways we never expected it to?"

Life in today's world can be at times so complicated and the challenges so overwhelming, they tend to be beyond our individual capacity to resolve them. Have you ever been in that place where you feel like the situations you are in, that you've gotten in over your head? You've tried and tried all within your power to change the situation but the more you try the worst it gets? You get to a place where all you have left to say is five words...

"Lord, I Need Your Help!"

This is not a passive cry. It's an urgent plea for <u>urgent assistance</u>. When you say Lord, I need your help you are asking for him to make the situation easier by offering aid, by offering support, and by offering relief. We all need Relief at some point. We need some burdens removed. We need our load to become lighter. We just need some alleviation. Lord, I Need Your HELP!

I want to encourage you today and let you know HELP IS ON THE WAY! Jeremiah 33:3 says – *"Call unto me and I will answer thee and show thee great and mighty things which thou knowest not of."* Be reassured in knowing that when you call unto The Lord, he will come to see about you and will strengthen and aid you through your trouble. God **IS** your refuge and strength a very present **HELP** in trouble. (Psalm 46:1 KJV)

> ***My Prayer:*** *In the name of Jesus, as life takes it daily course, I am depending solely on God to get me through every situation for I know that I can not do it, but God can.*

God Gets the Glory!

Day 16

$\mathcal{T}$he devil has a way to convince us that we have missed our blessings. He will play with your mind and make us feel like we have missed our time, or like our deliverance will never come. He will deceive us in to thinking that God has forgotten about us. He will make us feel like God doesn't love us. He will make us feel like it's too late for a turnaround in our homes, too late for healing in our bodies, too late for restoration to our families, too late for our churches to thrive, and too late for us to become all that we are supposed to be in him. So we feel defeated. But I want to encourage you in realizing, **It is Not Too Late**!

God has an appointed place and time for your deliverance, for your turn around, and for your coming out party. He's allowed uncomfortable things to happen, he's allowed the hurtful things to take place, he's allowed people to leave our lives, and he's allowed sickness to touch our bodies. He's allowed all these things to happen so that through each of these situations we will give God all The Glory!

Let your focus and your faith abide in the power and might of your God to see you through and He will get the glory.

> ***My Prayer:*** *In the name of Jesus, I declare that what the enemy meant for bad, God means for my good and I will give God all of the Glory!*

Finish What You've Started

Day 17

Galatians 5:7 (KJV) Ye did run well; who did hinder you that ye should not obey the truth?

The Apostle Paul is talking to the Galatians. They had been so full of joy and of love in their belief. Then they begin to turn their ears from the Truth to listen to erroneous or false teaching. The false apostles hindered them by doing all they could to turn them away from the right way…from the Truth.

What is hindering you? Is it your career or your job? You're so busy that you have lost sight of what is first. Is it your low self-image of yourself? Is it your present circumstance? What has hindered you? You were doing good, on fire, and zealous. You were determined, committed, focused, and dedicated. But something has come in and got you off your game.

Who stopped your Christian progress?

The race isn't given to the fastest or to the one that's the strongest, but to the one that endures until the end. The one that perseveres, the one that pushes through, the one that pushes despite circumstances, in the midst of adverse situations, that is the one who will win.

We must understand that the life of a Christian is a race that must be ran until the end. Christianity is far more than a verbal profession, there's an action that is required. Run the race. Endure the process. Overcome the obstacles. Finish the race and Win.

> *My Prayer:* In the name of Jesus, I declare that I not be distracted now will I allow anything or anyone to hinder my Christian Progress. I am built to win.

Re-present Christ

Day 18

2 Corinthians 5:20 (NIV) We are therefore Christ's ambassadors, as though God were making his appeal through us. We implore you on Christ's behalf; Be reconciled to God.

𝒯he world is looking for men and women to stand up and re-present Christ the correct way because so many people have misrepresented him. And we can do so by walking in Integrity. Integrity can be defined as being free from moral misconduct or free from an influence that goes against what is right to do. Integrity is doing the right thing even in private settings. People are always watching and you may be the only representation of Christ that some people will ever know; therefore, you have to ensure that you consistent and whole. There are so many people that are so impressionable and will go with whatever is popular. No longer are there standards, no longer are there convictions and there aren't many willing to stand for right when everyone is sitting down.

If you don't have integrity or consistency, you can be up today and down tomorrow. So many people rely on their gifts and talents, but your gift can get you there, but it is your character and integrity that will keep you where your gift has taken you. Re-present Christ in a manner that will make him smile and know that people are always watching you.

> ***My Prayer:*** *In the name of Jesus, I declare that I will always walk with integrity and good character so that I can ensure that I can represent Christ and make him smile.*

The Call to Make Disciples

Day 19

We are all called to "make disciples." A disciple is a "learner." One who is teachable, one who is disciplined. Being teachable and being disciplined are probably two of the greatest deficits within the body of Christ because in order to be teachable you have to be willing to be submitted.

Many believers are followers of Jesus, but not too many are true disciples. Jesus is the master disciple maker. So we have an example to follow. He invested his life into twelve men for three and a half years so that they, in turn could transmit that life to others.

1. He showed them who the Father was..
2. He taught them him to have a growing relationship with the Father.
3. He taught them to pray
4. He taught them to understand the Scriptures.
5. He taught them to minister with power.
6. He taught them to walk in humility and love.

Jesus described his ministry best in Luke 4:18-19: The Spirit of The Lord is upon me because he hath anointed me too preach the gospel to the poor; he hath sent me to heal the broken-hearted, to preach deliverance to the captives and recovering of sight to the blind, to set at liberty them that are bruised to preach the acceptable year of The Lord.

Later on in John 17:18, The Lord's disciples were sent out to do the same thing.

1. To preach the gospel and heal the sick
2. To reveal the character and love of the Father
3. To convince others of Divinity of Jesus
4. To disciple people in their personal relationships with God and his word.

Our calling as The Lord's disciples is exactly the same as that of Jesus and his original disciples.

Disciples do more than merely believe; they obey The Lord, they adhere to His ways. Making disciples requires teaching, mentoring and modeling the lifestyle of Jesus. It's not just the informing of facts; it is the imparting of life!

My Prayer: *In the Name of Jesus, I declare that I will be live a life of discipleship. I understand that it is my purpose to go out and allow my life to reflect that of Christ and it is my desire to fulfill that purpose.*

My War is Not With You

Day 20

$\mathcal{J}$t should come as no surprise to the believer, to the Christian that we are engaged in a great spiritual battle. It is very apparent that satan is the enemy of God and that he actively seeks to oppose God, his purpose and his people.

The sad thing is that there are some of us who don't even know that there is a war going on. And the ones who are still oblivious to that fact they make easy prey for the enemy. Christians should know that we are in the midst of a great spiritual struggle although many seem not to believe and even more distressing is the fact that many who consider themselves "in the war" do not understand the nature of Satan's schemes, of the weapons which he employs, or of the weapons that God has provided for our defense.

Why are we in war? We have to understand that when we came to faith in Christ by his grace we were delivered from Satan's kingdom the "kingdom of darkness" and made of citizens in the kingdom of light we were made citizens of the Kingdom of God. Our salvation caused us no longer to be the enemies of God, but at the same time resulted in us becoming the enemies of Satan. So this is why he aggressively attacks us by any means possible. He attacks our faith by making us feel like we made the wrong decision when we told The Lord yes; he attacks our bodies so that we won't be physically able to do God's work. He attacks our minds to make us feel like we are defeated, makes us feel like God has forgotten about us, makes us feel like things are not going to get any better but he is a liar. Satan couldn't tell the truth if he wanted to. His job is to steal, kill and destroy and he doesn't stop doing his job. He may take a break for a season but he is constantly trying to find a way to destroy the people of God.

One of the greatest things the enemy hates and fights against is unity. The Bible says where there is unity there is strength, if one can chase a thousand then how much more can we do if we are on one accord on the same page?

My Prayer: In the name of Jesus, I ask God to give me the strength and the boldness to withstand the tricks of Satan. With God, I know that the enemy will not win despite the approach that he tries to take.

The Lord is Concerned About You

Day 21

The Lord will perfect that which concerneth me: thy mercy O Lord endureth for ever. -Psalm 138:8

*A*m I in the will of God? What is God's will for my life? Am I where I'm suppose be? These are important questions to ask because being in the will of God is important in being a loyal follower and servant of The Lord.

But I want to encourage you today that if you are a believer, If you are seriously trying to follow Christ, you are not living in purposeful rebellion to The Lord and you're trying your best to honor him by honoring his word with your life each day, then God knows your heart. He knows your desire to please him. The message I want you to hear and receive today loud and clear is: **BE AT PEACE, YOUR LIFE IS IN GOD'S HANDS**, everything that concerns you God is concerned about. He said in his word that he will perfect those things that concerns us.

Which means:

1. The Lord will fulfill his purpose in your life.
2. The Lord will work out his plans for your
3. The Lord will accomplish what concerns you.
4. The Lord will do everything for me.

He will complete what he has begun. He will not say he is with you and then abandon you. He will not promise you to save you and then fail to fulfill his promise. He will not convert a soul and then leave it to perish.

Grace will complete what grace begins.

Phillipians 1:6 *"Being confident of this very thing that he which hath begun a good work in you will perform it until the day of Jesus Christ."*

When the thoughts come to your mind of feeling confused and misplaced and you start questioning your purpose, recognize that Satan is planting those seeds of doubt in your mind. Remember Satan is a liar, he can't tell the truth if he wanted to. So it's his job to keep you confused and questioning yourself you will never fulfill your purpose in God. As long as you don't know who you are and who you belong to, he has influence over your life. As soon as you come into the revelation that you belong to God, you're the property of Jesus Christ. You're in GOD'S HANDS! SATAN HAS NO POWER over you! He only has what you allow him to have.

Satan wants you to believe that you are out of God's will, that you aren't where God really wants you and doing what God really wants you to be doing. Satan is so nasty that he will even lie to those who serve The Lord and tell you that you are out of God's will. Don't listen to the lies of Satan! Don't let him rob you of your peace and joy in serving Christ. God wants you to be free to serve him and not bound up, confused and depressed, whether you are in the will of God or not.

God talks to his children and if you're in relationship, you are able to hear him. God speaks:
1. By His word
2. Through your time of prayer
3. Through others
4. Through circumstances

When God wants you to do something for him he will tell you. God places in us his passions and his desires.

I want to encourage you that **YOU ARE RIGHT WHERE GOD WANTS YOU TO BE!** God is always tweaking us, moving us a little to the left, a little to the right but for the most part you are right where God wants you. You can rest in that truth knowing that the will of The Lord shall prevail.

You may not know specifically what the plan and purpose is for your life. But we can have the assurance that as long as we are living in obedience to The Lord, doing our best to follow his word, yielding to His spirit. Then you are right where God wants you to be.

Psalm 37:23 says, "The steps of a good man are ordered by The Lord and he delighteth in his way."

My Prayer: *In the name of Jesus, I declare that Satan will not deter me from what God has ordained for me no matter how hard he may try. I will continue to walk boldly in the life God has designed for me. I am grateful that God took the time to place purpose within me, and I will pray that He continues to give me the grace to endure all odds.*
In Jesus Name I pray, Amen.

Acknowledgments

$\mathcal{J}$ am very grateful and thankful to God for blessing me with great people in my life that ensure I fulfill my God-given purpose. I have the best team in the world. They are definitely the A-squad, what would I do without you all.

Thank you to my assistant, "Ladybug" Martrina Williams, you are definitely God sent and like everyone says we are like synchronized swimmers. You just know my moves without me even saying. I love you! Kenya Lewis, you have been with me from the beginning. Thank you for managing my schedule and for keeping me all together. I love you!

To the B.A.D. squad, Benita Austin, Amber Burwell, and Danielle Ludy, what can I say, you all definitely know how to bring my vision into fruition. I am looking forward to the day to be able to bless you all the way that I desire to. To my Ruth, Tiffany Thomas, you impacted my life in such a short time, it's as if you have been with me all of the time. Thank you for making my life so much easier. I love you!

To "Auntie Nanny", Katrina Johnson, I am so grateful that God has allowed you to come and care for my precious babies. You do it with great joy, it's a blessing to be able to have someone to cover and care for my children while I do God's work. For all of those that serve on Shavon Sellers

Ministry team, thank you so much for all that you do. I love you!

Lastly, to all those that have covered me in prayer throughout the years without me even knowing, thank you and I love you!

Shavon Sellers Ministries

PRAYER AT NOON EST

**JOIN US EVERY TUESDAY
CALL 218.339.8542
& KEY IN 7777#**

NOON-EST - 11:00AM-CST * 10:00 AM-MST & 9:00 AM-PST

FOR UPDATES | ITINERARY | PRODUCTS GO TO

www.shavonsellers.org

FOLLOW US ON:

34613117R00035

Made in the USA
Charleston, SC
13 October 2014